CELTIC
MYTHS

CELTIC
MYTHS

Retold by
Sam McBratney

Illustrated by
Stephen Player

MACDONALD YOUNG BOOKS

To Maggie, ma belle-soeur, S.M.

First published in Great Britain in 1997 by Macdonald Young Books

Paperback edition first published in 1999 by Macdonald Young Books,
an imprint of Wayland Publishers Limited
61 Western Road
Hove
East Sussex
BN3 1JD

Find Macdonald Young Books on the Internet at http://www.myb.co.uk

Designer   Dalia Hartman
Editor   Lisa Edwards
Illustrator   Stephen Player

Text © Sam McBratney 1997
Illustrations © Macdonald Young Books 1997

Printed and bound in Portugal by Edições ASA

A CIP catalogue record for this book is available from the British Library

ISBN: 0 7500 2858 0

CONTENTS

The stories in this book come from a time before history – a time when nothing was written down.

The people of that time see mystery and magic in everything around them. The wild boar you are hunting might have been someone you used to know in its former life. The crow sitting over there on a branch might be a visitor from the Otherworld of spirits. There are magical trees; stones with strange powers; spears that cannot miss their target. In the strange world of these stories poor men become kings and people are transformed into creatures of the animal kingdom. Come with me now to the time of the spoken word. There are heroes to be talked about when the nights are long and the winter fires are burning...

THE HOUND OF ULSTER

Our first story is about the greatest of Ireland's early heroes.
He was called Setanta as a child. This story tells how he
*came to be known as "Cuchulainn".**

When Setanta was still a child he was sent into the north of Ireland to live at the court of King Conor. Boys were often fostered in those days. The court of King Conor was really a school for young warriors where they learned the arts of wrestling and archery, hunting and hawking, and also how to play the royal game of chess. Each boy's ambition was to become one of Conor's famous Red Branch Warriors.

At first glance Setanta was nothing much to look at. Many of the other boys seemed bigger and stronger than he was. And yet, anyone watching the boys at play would have seen one who could run faster and further than the rest, and one who

* Cuchulainn is pronounced Koo-hoo-lin

had more skill with the sling and the sword than any of the others. This was Setanta. He trained hard to learn the arts of war, as if he knew that in the heat of real battle a warrior did not get a second chance, because his first mistake had killed him.

One day the boys were at play when a group of horsemen came down the hill towards them. King Conor and his Red Branch Warriors were on their way to a feast at the home of Cullan the blacksmith.

They stopped to watch the game between the teams of boys. It soon became obvious that Setanta was the best player on the field. Not for the first time, Conor was struck by the boy's amazing energy. And by his will to win! The King remembered a prophecy which had been made at the time of the boy's birth: *the name of this child shall be in the mouths of all men, and poets shall sing of his deeds.*

'Setanta!' Conor called out. 'We're visiting tonight at Cullan's house. There's a place at table for you if you want to come. Good red meat, boy. Good red wine.'

Fergus Roy, one of the Red Branch Warriors, laughed out loud as he nudged his horse forward. 'The boy is no bigger than a nettle, Conor. He's too young for good red meat and good red wine. It would be wasted.'

'One of these days I'll spill *your* good red blood, Fergus,' Setanta shouted back.

This was met by a roar of merriment from the mounted warriors; but the King was impatient to be away. 'Well? Are you coming or not, boy? We want to get to Cullan's place before dark.'

'We haven't won the game yet, Conor.'

The little cub must have his victory! thought Conor. Oh well, perhaps it was no bad thing. 'Finish it, then. We'll leave a horse for you and you can follow after.'

Conor and the Red Branch Warriors made their way to the hill where Cullan lived. The huts on the crest of the hill were surrounded by a wooden fence. It was getting late, so Cullan had already gathered his animals into the stockade. A sign of the times, thought Conor. You could never tell when a raiding party might come out of the woods and make off with your cattle.

They were met by Cullan himself. At his side, held tight on a strap, a ferocious beast slabbered at the mouth as if it had not been fed for a week. This was Halfwolf. The dog was famous throughout the land. It would attack any living thing that moved.

Conor, dismounting, embraced his old friend. 'So how are things for the best sword-beater in the land?'

'Oh, quiet enough. But I have a spear to show you, Conor, that will pin any man in the world to the nearest tree.' Cullan raised his voice to the Red Branch Warriors, 'Come through the gate! I like to make the place safe at night.'

'Keep a good tight hold on that crazy animal, Cullan,' Fergus said.

'She's all right, she knows you're friends – don't you, my lady?' Cullan smiled fondly at Halfwolf. 'She wouldn't be any use to me if she was a quiet little pet, would she? Every thieving beggar knows that if he comes near this place, the dog will eat his heart out. Is everyone here, Conor?'

'Yes, we're all here. Fergus is looking forward to good red meat and good red wine.'

'Go inside, then, there's plenty of both. I'll be with you in no time.'

When the others had gone inside, Cullan made sure that the hurdle gate was shut. Then, letting the dog off the strap, he whispered into its ear. 'There you go, Halfwolf. It's over to you, my lady. Guard us well; anything strange you don't like the smell of – it's all yours.'

• • •

The game was over. Setanta did not hurry his horse on the way to Cullan's house, for this was the time of day-becoming-night when nothing could be seen clearly. There was no point in riding headfirst into the branch of a tree.

The hurdle gate was up when he arrived. No matter, thought Setanta - he would climb the gate, open it from the inside and let his horse through. Such, at any rate, was his plan. But as soon as his feet landed within the wooden stockade, a bounding, shifting shape came out of the night towards him. The speed of the creature's attack surprised and shocked him. At first he had no idea what it was; it was like the rising up again of some terror he had buried in a long-forgotten dream. Then Setanta saw the teeth and the steaming breath of the creature. He heard the low snarl of rage in its throat become a roar, and he knew that the hound of Cullan was almost upon him.

• • •

Inside the main hut, where the meal had just begun, they heard the same roar. Cullan glanced towards the door in alarm.

'It's Halfwolf! Something is after the animals.'

Then Conor swept to his feet, his face as pale as death in the rushlights. 'Ah, the boy!'

'What boy?' cried Cullan.

'Curse me for a fool, Cullan, I forgot about the *boy*. He was to follow after us. Call it off!'

'But Conor,' Cullan cried out as the King rushed past him, 'whoever that is there can be no hope for him! You said everyone was *here*. Ye gods and stars, the dog is only doing what it must do.'

Conor raced out of the hut and across open ground, towards the shapes near the gate. *The dog is twice the boy's weight*, he was thinking. *There can be no hope for him. None. The brute is a born killer.* Conor could not bear to see what he knew he must see by the light of torches now arriving.

The Red Branch Warriors saw the dog in the air above Setanta's head as he flung it against the pillar of the gate. It slumped to the ground in a limp heap. Even as it tried to struggle to its feet again, Setanta thrust his javelin into its body,

and it lay quite still.

After some moments Fergus turned to Conor with a whisper. 'It's dead. He's killed the hound of Cullan, almost with his bare hands. How can this be, Conor? Just thinking of that beast gave full-grown men nightmares!'

'I know. The boy is . . . unusual.'

And now Cullan came to kneel at the body of his dog, from where he looked up with a kind of desperation. 'I'm glad the boy is alive, Conor, everyone knows I would wish no one of yours any harm. But this animal was a loyal servant and a friend to me.' He pulled out the javelin and returned it to Setanta in a sullen way. 'And now she's dead. Who will protect me now from thieves and robbers? Everyone knows the times we live in!'

Setanta spoke. 'Have you no other dogs?'

'I have a pup of six months. One of *hers*.'

'Well then,' Setanta went on, 'here is my offer to you, Cullan. Raise the pup as you raised this one – to be your servant and your friend. And while the pup is growing I will take Halfwolf's place. I will protect your property and your animals until the pup is old enough to do the job that Halfwolf did. *Me* for the dog.' He glanced at the King. 'If Conor agrees.'

Conor nodded. 'What do you say, Cullan? The boy can't do fairer than that, you've seen for yourself what a hound he can be.'

'Well . . . It sounds like a reasonable bargain.'

'And the little twig probably eats less than a dog,' laughed Fergus. 'We'll have to find a suitable name for you, boy – no more 'Setanta'. You are now Cuchulainn, which means the Hound of Cullan! Can you howl like a wolf in the night?'

With whoops and cries, and howling like wolves in the night, the Red Branch Warriors returned to the meal which still awaited them in the main hut. Conor remained alone for some moments, reflecting on what he had seen. The prophecy was true, he saw that now. The boy would become the greatest of the Red Branch Warriors, and poets would sing the song of this champion down the ages. Cuchulainn. A good name, it had a ring to it.

And in time the Hound of Cullan would become the Hound of Ulster.

THE CHILDREN OF LIR

*Many stories of long ago are tales of transformation, in which
people are changed into a different form. What happened
to the Children of Lir is one of the most haunting
examples of this kind of story.*

The old stories say that in Ireland long ago there lived a race of beings who
looked like people, but had the powers of gods. One of these beings was Lir. Lir
had a daughter called Fionula*, a son called Hugh, and twin boys called Fiachra**
and Conn. At the birth of the twins Lir's wife died, and the loss of her was heart-
breaking. Lir grieved not only for himself, but also for his children, who must
now grow up without the loving care of their mother.

After a time Lir married again. His second bride, Aoife***, was the sister of his
dead wife. It may be that Aoife reminded Lir of the woman he had lost; certainly

* Fionula is pronounced Fin-oola
** Fiachra is pronounced Fee-akra
*** Aoife is pronounced Eef-eh

he believed that she would care for his children and add to the happiness and security of their early years.

This did not happen. Aoife had no children of her own. She became jealous of Lir's intense love for his children. Jealousy is a powerful force, and it made her wish Fionula and the boys were dead. Only then would Lir give to her the affection that she longed for and felt she deserved.

Planning murder is not easy. Unable to persuade her servants to get rid of the children for her, Aoife took them away to the lonely Lake of Darvra, where she intended to arrange an "accident" for them. But at the last she could not bring herself to kill them and instead, using magic that she knew of, she changed the children of Lir into four white swans.

The transformation of the children into wild birds was not quite complete. They had lost their human shape, but still had the power to speak, and think, and feel. Strangest of all, perhaps, the enchantment gave them a wonderful gift of song.

'Why are you doing this to us?' asked Fionula. 'Don't you know how much our father will miss us?'

'He will be so angry with you if you go home alone,' cried Hugh.

This reminder of Lir's love for the children made Aoife raise her voice in anger. 'Be quiet and hear me! For three hundred years you shall remain here on Darvra Lake, and three hundred years on the Sea of Moyle, and three hundred years by the island of Glora. For nine hundred years I give you the enchanted shape of swans - until the woman of the south marries the man of the north, and the enchantment ends.'

Aoife turned and ran from the lake. She believed that she had parted Lir and his children for ever; but as she made her way home she began to hear the sound of the four swans sweetly singing. She shut out the sound as best she could, and hurried home.

She had her story ready and she told it well. Lir heard how his children had bathed in the lake and gone too far from the shallow edge. They would not listen to Aoife. The current had swept them away and they had drowned among the reeds and weeds. With tears in her eyes Aoife asked for Lir's understanding and

forgiveness, but she had done all that anyone could do to save his Fionula and her little brothers.

Lir's sorrow was terrible to see. And with the grief came a great dark rage, for he suspected his wife of treachery. That one child might drown he could accept – perhaps – as a dreadful tragedy; but not all four of them at the same time. He rushed away from the wretched Aoife to see the lake for himself.

When Lir arrived by the shore of the lake there was no wind to speak of. Across the smooth water of Darvra four swans swam towards him under a pale moon. The one who had been his lovely Fionula told him of their enchantment, and then one of the twins spoke.

'Can't you make us the way we were again, Father?'

Lir bowed his head in desperation. 'I don't think I can. Whatever power she used, I cannot match it. Oh, blind and useless fool that I am, I should have seen the truth about her. I could have stopped her!'

'We mustn't mind too much,' said Fionula, seeing how her father blamed himself for what had happened. 'We can still remember how happy we used to be. You must come and see us often, Father, and you'll see that things will not be so bad for us.'

Lir caressed the strange new forms of his lost children until he could bear to stay no longer. He, too, heard the sweet song of the swans as he returned home.

It soon became clear to Aoife that her plan had failed. Far from transferring his affections to her, Lir could hardly bear her company. He brought the story of her evil to the King of the Gods, whose name was Bov. Bov spoke to Aoife in this way:

'Aoife, where are the children of Lir?'

'Drowned, my lord, in the Lake of Darvra.'

'Who are the four swan-children, then, that swim on the Lake of Darvra? I have seen them Aoife, with my own eyes, I have touched them with my hand and I have heard them sing. If it was in my power to bring them back I would do it gladly, but the enchantment you laid on them must remain – as the enchantment that I now lay upon *you* shall remain!'

No magic that Aoife knew could save her now. She, too, lost her human form

and became a demon of the air. Banished, she flew out of the land on great dark wings, without the gifts of speech or song or the power to do evil again.

•   •   •

Three hundred years went by. It was time for the swan-children to leave Darvra and fly to the Sea of Moyle on the northern coast. In that wild place they were thrashed by wind and tide. The power of thought and speech were gifts they could have done without, for they felt as keenly as any exile the loss of their native land, and the song of the swan-children was a sorrowful thing to hear. Fionula, the eldest of the four, would gather the others under her wings during the winter frosts. 'One day we shall be ourselves again,' she told them, 'and we shall return to the Land of Youth.'

After three hundred years they flew towards the Atlantic Ocean for the third stage of their ordeal. As the years went by they found little to comfort them in that desolate place, but one day they heard a sound which they had never heard before. It was the sound of a bell. It came from the tiny church of a hermit who lived close by. The swan-children made friends with the hermit, who listened to their story and their song, and taught them to say the prayers he knew.

The final period of three hundred years was coming to an end. Fionula and her brothers longed to see again the Hill of the White Field, where their father lived. How was he after all this time, they wondered.

The palace of Lir was still there in the White Field, but the swan-children could not see it as they flew over; they saw only rough land overgrown with weeds. It was as if time had changed everything, even their way of seeing. Fionula and her brothers did not know it then, but they would never be the way they were and they would never return to the Land of Youth. They flew back to the island of Glora to wait for the end of their enchantment.

Their long wait was coming to an end. A princess from the southern part of Ireland was to wed a chieftain from the north. As a wedding gift she asked for the four swans of Glora, whose wonderful singing she had heard of. The chieftain tried to bribe the hermit to give him the swans. When the hermit refused to let them go, the chief settled the matter by dragging off the swans in silver chains; then he brought them before his bride-to-be and called on them to sing.

The sorrows of the children of Lir were almost over. Not a note could they sing for the chieftain's bride. Before the eyes of everyone present they changed again, and took on the appearance of human beings. But they were old. The sudden presence of these four frail and shrunken bodies with their withered limbs caused the bride to run away in panic, but the hermit understood what was happening. Now at the end of their days the children of Lir had become human souls, and he baptized them before they died.

'You must lay us in one grave,' Fionula whispered to him, 'so that I can shelter my brothers as I used to do when we were on the Sea of Moyle.'

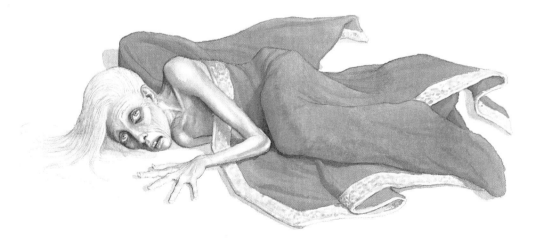

A ROYAL SECRET

There was once a king in Ireland who had a head of the wildest hair you could imagine. When you saw him coming down the path he looked like a whin bush on the move. His name was Labraidh.*

The hair was a torment to him in the summer-time, for it kept in the heat during those long warm nights. He would toss and turn in his bed trying to get comfortable, and then sit up to scratch furiously by the light of the moon.

'Majesty,' his close friends used to say, 'would you not wear your hair in a plait at the back rather than walking about looking … you know, looking …' And then they would pause. You couldn't very well say 'looking long and shaggy' to a king.

* Labraidh is pronounced Larry

Once a year the King had to get his hair cut, and if you think about it you'll understand why. Half the time his crown wouldn't stay on his head; it slipped off and rolled across the palace floor like a hoop. And when it *did* stay on his head, it nestled down into the bush and just looked ridiculous. The whole point about a crown is that it should be seen. One morning the King woke up convinced that he had fleas, and called for a barber.

'Majesty,' said his most trusted adviser, 'can you not wait a little longer? It's still only the month of May, and we could have a long hot summer. Postpone your haircut until July.'

'I won't,' said the King. 'My scalp is being eaten by every bug under the sun. Fetch me a barber!'

Word then went out across the land that King Labraidh was about to have his hair cut. Strong men trembled in their shoes, for any man who cut the King's hair was never seen again. He disappeared without trace, and no one knew where, or why.

This year the choice of the King's soldiers fell on a lad named Brian, who was brought to the castle and supplied with a fine pair of silver scissors. Then the King led him through several doors, each one with two strong bolts and two strong locks, and sat down in front of a mirror.

'Start cutting,' said the King. 'And mind you go easy!'

So Brian began to prune the extraordinary thatch below him. While the cutting went on, Labraidh's eyes never left the mirror in front of him. He was waiting for that special look which sooner or later came over the face of every barber he had ever known – and sure enough, it came. Brian let out a cry, a sort of strangled squawk of astonishment and horror, and staggered backwards as if he'd taken a good one on the chin. The silver scissors slipped from his grasp to the floor.

'Well?' said Labraidh. 'What have you seen?'

'N-nothing, Majesty,' came the whispered reply.

'I'll ask you again. What have you seen? Come, boy, give me an answer.'

Brian cleared his throat. 'It's . . . It's your *ears.*'

'What about them?'

'You've got horse's ears!' howled Brian.

'Correct. I have ears like a horse. Now carry on with your work. My men will be in shortly to take you away.'

'But I won't tell anyone,' Brian burst out desperately, 'I swear I will never say a word to a living soul!'

'Too big a risk, I'm afraid,' said Labraidh. 'We can't have this getting out. The people will laugh at me, you see. Pick up the scissors like a good fellow and we'll find you a nice island far away where you'll be perfectly happy.'

That evening a woman came to see the King. She spoke up to him fearlessly, saying that he was taking away her only son, her only helping hand about the house - and her a poor widow into the bargain. 'A son is a woman's life's work, Majesty,' she went on in a voice that was steady with the truth, 'and only a tyrant would fail to see that. You say that you love your people, and maybe you do, but I tell you this - you make it hard for them to love you.'

The King (who was listening to these words with his head in a hood) began to think about what the woman had said, and eventually went down to the prison-hole to speak to young Brian.

'All right, you can go. But you must never speak my secret, not to your mother, not to your wife when you marry, not to your children when they are born. No person must know. This is the bargain you have made - to carry my secret to the grave with you.'

'Not a living soul, Majesty, never!' agreed Brian.

But as time went on, the secret in some mysterious way began to weigh on Brian's mind. It never left him. He thought of it when he closed his eyes at night, and it was the first thing into his mind when the morning came. He became listless and moody. At meal-times he picked through his food without ever eating anything of substance. Soon Brian was hardly fit for a day's work, so his poor mother sent for a healer to come and look at him.

The healer listened to all that Brian had to say, and began to nod. 'You must tell me what you know, boy, or I see no hope for you. Some secrets are too big for one person and this is obviously one of them.'

'You're no help,' Brian complained bitterly. 'I have given my oath, I am honour bound. I can tell no other person what I know and there's an end of it!'

'Then take your secret deep into the woods and tell it there. Stand by the tall crack willow tree and say aloud what you know. No living person will hear you - but you will be heard. Oh yes, you will most certainly be heard.'

Brian didn't like to press the healer too closely on this matter, for he took as little interest as possible in the Otherworld of spirits. All the same, since the secret was driving him out of his mind, he decided to visit the crack willow tree and see what happened.

At first the words wouldn't come and he could hardly get the secret out of his mouth. Eventually he managed to whisper, 'Our King Labraidh . . . He's got . . . He's got . . . He's got ears like a horse!'

All at once Brian felt as free and easy as the breeze that blew in and out of the grasses and the late summer flowers. As he pranced about full of the joys of life once more, he shouted: 'He's got ears like a horse. He has! Great big whoppers. Horse's ears, that's what he's got. GREAT KING LABRAIDH, HORSY EARS!' From that time forward Brian's life was normal again, and he never had much to do with secrets from then until his dying day.

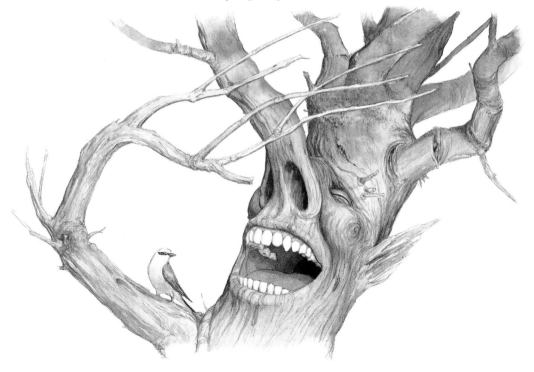

A few months after these events a great wind began to blow, and down in the woods the leaves of the crack willow began to rustle. The rustling spread to the wild grasses growing by the streams, and was taken up by the rushes in the wetlands and by the corn growing in the cultivated fields.

The people there paused, listening to the wind in the corn. It seemed to say, 'The King has horse's ears, the King has horse's ears . . .'

Well, the secret was out. But nobody dared to tell the King, who continued to wear his hair like a whin bush, and itch and scratch in the royal bed.

Until a day came when the King's musician broke his harp, and set out for the forest to cut himself a bit of wood for a new one. He chose to cut from a fine crack willow tree that grew in the depths of the wood. The new harp was made – just in time to entertain the King's guests at an important banquet.

As soon as the harpist began to play, his music was sweet and mellow and pleasing to the ear; but there was something else present besides the notes that his skilful fingers plucked from the instrument – something within the music but not of it, a rustling blend of meadow-voices whispering their small refrain . . . 'The King has horse's ears, the King has horse's ears . . .'

There was uproar. People lay across the tables, helpless as babies, with tears of laughter rolling down their faces. King Labraidh swept to his feet, truly formidable in his rage, except that he had to hold his wobbly crown on his head with one hand.

The whole world seemed to be having fun at his expense, and not a thing could he do about it. Well, thought Labraidh, I can laugh with them, or I can cry alone.

He chose to laugh.

It was a strange thing, but after that night a new spirit seemed to be over the land. The exiled barbers were recalled and returned to their families. The King had a great horror of secrets now, and he governed the country openly and honestly, hiding nothing from the people, neither good news nor bad. Even in old age he would sometimes get down from his horse and have a joke with children in the country lanes. And the children would run away home to their parents, shouting, 'We'll all have good luck! We saw King Labraidh's ears!'

THE MESTER STOORWORM

*Mester means "master". Stories are told about other great worms,
but this one was the daddy of them all.*

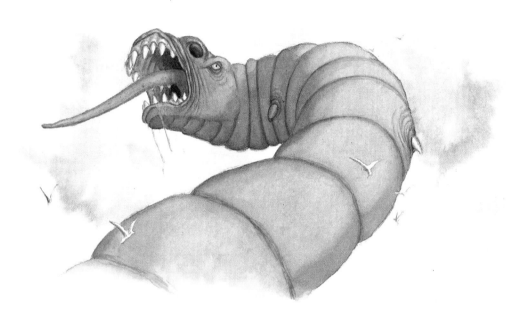

The Mester Stoorworm of long ago was a frightful beast. You might have in your
head a picture of the worst monster ever thought of, but I can tell you this: the
Stoorworm was worse. No nightmare that was ever dreamed could compare with
it. For a start, the Stoorworm was so big you couldn't see all of it at once, for it
stretched to the far horizon, and then went on some more. The bit you *could* see
was so awful that the people who spied it either bolted down the nearest hole or
fainted clean away.

   One day the Stoorworm swam up a river in Scotland. It swam and it swam
until the river got narrow and it could swim no more, then it poked up its ugly
big head and let it fall upon the land. The thump of that head coming down was
heard and felt both near and far.

It began to eat. It ate the corn, it ate the cows, it swallowed people whole, and if the people were riding horses it swallowed them horse and all! Nothing was safe. Not even buildings. It chewed the thatch off the roofs. A flick of its tail could sink a fishing boat or demolish a harbour wall. And the vile breath from the creature's mouth caused trees that had been growing for a hundred years to die. Faced by hunger, homelessness and worse, the good people turned to the King for help.

'Majesty, save us please,' the cry went up, 'save us and our children from the Mester Stoorworm and ruin!'

The King gathered up his bravest soldiers and sent them out to fight the beast. Among the crowd who watched the battle from the top of a far hill was a farmer and his seven sons, the youngest of whom was called Assipattle. They saw the Stoorworm eat all the King's horses and all the King's men, and afterwards lick its awful lips.

'If I could go down there and fight that Stoorworm,' cried Assipattle, 'I would give it something to think about. And I'd make short work of it, too.'

'Hold your tongue and less of your boasting,' said his father with a sigh. The truth is that he regarded Assipattle as a good-for-nothing dreamer. 'You're not much use to us alive, boy, but you'll be no use at all if you're *dead*.'

The defeat of the soldiers was a blow to everyone's hopes. The King himself, convinced that only one thing could work against this monster, sent for the most famous sorcerer in the country.

'You must find me a plan,' said the King, 'to kill the Stoorworm by magic.'

'I don't know about killing it, Majesty,' replied the sorcerer. 'There may be a way to make it leave us alone, but I cannot bear to mention it.'

'And why not?' asked the King.

'We must offer up a sacrifice, Majesty. Someone loved by us all must be given to the Stoorworm, and then it will leave us in peace.'

'Who?' thundered the King.

'I dare not say.'

'Who is it, man – do you mean myself?'

'Worse, sire. I mean your only child. I mean your. . . your. . .'

Your 'daughter' was the word he feared to say, for the sorcerer knew that the Princess was not only heir to the King's throne, but also his very heart's joy.

'My Gemma?' breathed the King, seizing the sorcerer by the shoulders. 'You dare tell me I must give up the Princess Gemma!'

In a curious way, though, the King understood the power of the sorcerer's words. All things have their price. It was only natural that something pure and innocent must be used to drive out a terrible evil – somehow one cancelled out the other. But how he wished that someone else's daughter might be used!

'Very well,' he whispered. 'If that is the price, we must pay it. But not yet! There must surely be a better way!'

The King sent out messengers, and this is what they cried aloud in every town and village across the land:

'Hear the word and promise of his great majesty the King! Any person, no matter what his birth, who removes the curse of the Stoorworm shall have the Princess Gemma for a wife, and they shall rule the country together as your king and queen.'

It was a wonderful prize. Warriors, princes, shepherds, blacksmiths, farmers, fishermen, rogues and ne'er-do-wells and even wretched thieves with one foot upon the gallows – they thought about it deeply. A queen and a kingdom at a stroke! Then they thought about the Stoorworm and the idea went out of their heads.

When the King's messengers came to Assipattle's village they caused a great stir. Assipattle declared to his brothers that *he* would kill the Stoorworm, which made them angry, and they pelted him with pine cones the whole way home. They were fed up with Assipattle, who never did any work on the farm. While *they* went out in all weather, he lay about the chimney corner smelling of smoke and peat, stoking the fire, and making up stories in which he was always the great hero who saved the world from giants, trolls and witches.

His mother raced out to rescue him from his brothers when they got home. 'There's no need to go picking on him all the time,' she complained to her sons.

'It's all right, Mother,' said Assipattle, 'I could have fought every one of them if I'd wanted to. I could have knocked out all six of them with these fists.'

'Then why didn't you?' cried his brothers.

'Because I'm saving all my strength,' said Assipattle. 'For the Mester Stoorworm.'

Everyone smiled. They couldn't help it. Assipattle's father shoved him into the house, saying, 'Boy, you'll fight the Stoorworm when I make spoons from the horns of the moon.'

That night, Assipattle lay down as usual by the fire in the chimney corner. As quiet as a mouse he lay, but without closing his eyes. He had important work to do.

Sometime after midnight Assipattle crept out of the house, bringing with him a clay pot. And in the clay pot was a hot glow of burning embers from the fire. He set it into a boat by the shore, and began to row across the dark water.

At dawn the following day, the Princess was taken to the cliffs at the water's edge. No champion had come forward to challenge the Stoorworm, and it seemed that she must die. An unhappy crowd watched from a safe way back, and the King was with her. He had strapped around his waist the great sword of his fathers called Snickersnapper, although in his heart he did not believe that any weapon could help him or the Princess Gemma now.

In the early morning light, a small boat was seen approaching the Stoorworm.

This was Assipattle on the water, although no one knew it at the time. He steered for the mouth of the vile serpent, which rose before him like a newly discovered island. In the east, the sun came over the horizon, and Assipattle whispered, more to himself than to the monster, 'Waken up my beauty, morning has broken - time for a *yawn*!'

The great beast opened its mouth to taste the new morning. Then a tide of in-rushing water sucked Assipattle's boat into the cave of its jaws as if the boat were only a cork. On and on, down and down, Assipattle rode the gushing flow, until the throat narrowed and the keel of the boat wedged in something solid.

Now was the time to blow on the burning embers. '*Fire in the belly, Stoorworm,*' Assipattle whispered, as with his knife he cut a hole in a wall of flesh to hold the glowing wood and peat. The wood and peat, nourished by the creature's natural oils, grew into a flame. Assipattle stood back, satisfied. There was a fair fire already, and quite some heat. The overpowering smell reminded him of liver frying.

The Stoorworm, being so large, didn't realize for some time that he had a problem down below. But when he did, his body gave one heave and a mighty retch, and out of his mouth flew a horrible mixture of smoke, and old dinners, and smashed boat, and of course, Assipattle himself, who scrambled ashore and rushed up to the high, dry land as quickly as he could go.

The Stoorworm was turning and twisting fit to tie himself in knots. Anyone could see that he was on his last legs. Still thrashing and plunging horribly, he withdrew his loathsome presence out to sea, and sank beneath the boiling ocean.

Such scenes there were! People love a hero and they had a hero now, no doubt. The tumult was only interrupted briefly while the King placed one hand of his daughter's into one of Assipattle's. This showed that he meant to keep his promise.

That's how the Mester Stoorworm lived and died. Now and then Assipattle's father would look up at the horns of the moon, and marvel that he now had a king in the family. As for the Mester Stoorworm, what's left of him smoulders on. You may see him smoking still if you visit the hot geysers and burning mountains of Iceland.

A QUESTION FOR KING ARTHUR

King Arthur, like many kings of long ago, loved to hunt wild beasts through the woods that covered so much of the land in those days.

One day Arthur and his nobles startled a young stag at the edge of a forest, and soon they were in full cry after the fleeing animal. They were driven by the thrill of the chase, the excitement of the kill, and the prospect of good meat. But the stag was quick! Even Arthur, who was mounted on the best of his royal horses, could not follow it through the twists and turns of the forest paths; and he lost it.

By now it was late in the afternoon, and when Arthur looked around him he saw that he was alone in a place he did not know. Not only had he lost the stag; he had managed to lose himself into the bargain. As the night closed in, creating shadows and dark holes on every side, the King began to fear that he was doing nothing more than riding slowly round in circles. Then he came upon a woodsman making charcoal in a clearing.

'Is there a place nearby where I can spend the night?' Arthur asked him.

The woodsman pointed with a glowing ember. 'That path will take you to the castle-tower of the lord of these parts. His name is Gromersomer Joure. But if you go there, keep your wits about you, sir.'

'Why do you say that? Is this . . . Gromersomer Joure . . . no friend to strangers?'

'He's no friend to anybody,' grunted the woodsman, and returned to his business as though he'd said enough.

Presently Arthur came to a narrow bridge at the end of the path. Beyond the bridge loomed the great silhouette of the castle-tower, where lanterns flickered in the upper windows. Surely, thought Arthur, I will be safer in there than out here in the company of wolves and bears.

And indeed, the King could not find any immediate fault with the welcome he received from Baron Gromersomer Joure – he dined on the best of food and wine, and slept soundly in a bed stuffed with horsehair and feathers. Only in the morning did he learn that there was a price to be paid for such wonderful hospitality. His very life was in danger!

Gromersomer Joure was a strange man with a gruesome idea of fun. Over breakfast he explained to Arthur that he always asked his guests a question, and that if they did not answer the question correctly then they could not leave his castle alive.

'It's a little custom of mine, Majesty,' he went on. 'And you need not feel for your sword, for it is still where you left it last night – stuck into your mattress. In any case, there are too many of us for you, so accept your fate.'

'What is my question, then?' Arthur asked uneasily, for he was aware that he had stumbled into a deadly game.

'Simply this: What do women want most in all the world? That is what you must tell me on pain of death. It's not so difficult, is it? But . . .' and here Gromersomer Joure smiled across the table with blackened teeth '. . . do not rush to answer now. A king is a king, after all, and I will give you a year and a day to think it over.'

'And if I don't come back?' said Arthur.

'You will give me your word as a knight and a royal prince. And if you break your word then I will put a curse on you and yours that will last until the end of time. Goodbye, Majesty. You have one year and one day.'

Thus began for King Arthur a bizarre search. What do women want most in all the world? When he returned to his court he took advice from many people, but the answers he received were contradictory. Some said "magnificent clothes", "good looks" or "fine jewellery". Others favoured "a noble husband", "long life" or simply "happiness". As the months went by Arthur wondered which was the right answer, or at least, which was the answer that Gromersomer Joure wanted to hear? To help him decide he rode out one day to talk with a wise old hermit who lived in a cave.

The hermit gave the problem some thought before he spoke. 'Majesty, I would say that women want most of all a fire in the home, food on the table, and a child to care for. That is how I would answer.'

This seemed reasonable. But on the way home the King began to have doubts. Had the hermit not given him three answers instead of just one? And anyway, what could an old man who lived alone in a cave possibly know about the women of this world? He was thinking that the real answer still eluded him when a beggar woman stopped his horse on the road to Camelot, and asked to speak to him.

She was not a pretty sight. The clothes hung on her bent old back like rags and her skin was lumpy with warts. Under the fringe of her shawl only one good eye glittered: the other was an empty purple hole in her face. Everything about this creature suggested that a life of poverty and bad luck had unsettled her mind.

Arthur tossed her a coin. 'There you are. For bread and shelter,' he said.

'No,' she croaked. 'It's the riddle! I have the answer to the *riddle*. I'm the only one who can help you against the evil magic of Gromersomer Joure.'

No doubt she has heard some gossip, thought Arthur. 'Tell me the answer, then.'

'First agree to my price. If I tell you the answer he wants to hear, you must give me as wife to the noblest of your knights – I mean the one called Gawain.'

Arthur, who did not know whether to smile or to shudder at the thought of the handsome Gawain being married to this old wanderer of the roads, decided to humour her. 'Very well, you have the word of the King. Let me hear your answer. What do women most want in all the world?'

'They want their own way!' came the reply. 'That is what you must tell the Baron.' And then she was gone.

When the year and a day were over, Arthur returned to the castle-tower in the woods. Gromersomer Joure lost no time in demanding an answer from him.

'The truth is that I have many answers to your question,' said Arthur. 'After all, not every woman wants the same thing from life – nor every man either, if it comes to that.' And he repeated some of the common answers he had heard.

The Baron smiled his cruel, curling smile. 'Give me the answer I am looking for, Majesty, or pay the price.'

Then Arthur gave the answer that the beggar woman had told him to give: 'Their own way' - at which Gromersome Joure swept to his feet in the grip of a terrifying rage.

'Ah, my sister. Rag Nell!' he hissed. 'My hag of a *sister* has told you what to say.'

'The game is over,' said Arthur. 'By the rules you laid down, I owe you nothing.' And if I ever pass this way again, he was thinking, it will be at the head of an army to put an end to you and your questions.

Arthur went back to Camelot. He now had to explain to Gawain - whose fresh good looks made sweet young maidens sigh - that he must marry a wild thing of the road called Rag Nell.

Strangely enough, Gawain took the news well. He saw that Arthur had given his word to Rag Nell, and that he must marry her as a matter of honour. On their wedding night he resolved to treat her with courtesy and respect, for Gawain understood that age and decay are things which come to us all. As he kissed her once on the lips, Rag Nell was transformed before his eyes. Instead of a shrivelled old lady, he was in the presence of a beautiful girl with dancing hair and bright blue shining eyes.

'Thank you, my lord,' she said to him. 'You have lifted from me one half of the spell of ugliness that my brother cursed me with. I will be your loyal wife for as long as you want me.'

'*Half* the curse?' said the startled Gawain.

'Yes. I can only be the way you see me now for part of the day, and now you must choose. Would you rather have me ugly by day and beautiful by night, or the other way round?'

Gawain did not know what to think. Which would suit him best - a lovely wife by day, in company? Or at night when they were both alone?

'My lady, you may choose,' he said. 'It is you who must suffer this curse, and therefore it is only right that you should have your own way.'

As soon as he spoke Rag Nell threw up her arms with a cry of joy, for this was the answer that broke the other half of the spell her brother had put on her. From that time forward Rag Nell was her true self by day and by night, and Gawain treasured the wife that unselfishness and good manners had won for him.

THE LAND OF YOUTH

*Storytellers have always been fascinated by time. What is it?
Can human beings do anything to stop the passing of time?
My first memory of a story about time is the story of
Rip Van Winkle, who fell asleep for twenty years. Here
is another one, but much older.*

My name is Oisin.* If you could see me now, as I sit in the shade of oak trees, you would see nothing more or less than an old man whose life is almost over.

I am thinking about Time - how it is a force we cannot oppose. As surely as it withers the leaves above me it will part us all from our loved ones, for it knows no pity. If you are young and hearing my story, you have only to wait. It will write its lines in your face, too.

And yet, there is a place where Time has no dominion. I have been there, I have seen the Land of Youth called Tir Na nOg. The story I have to tell began one morning when I saw the rider on the white horse come over the lake.

* Oisin is pronounced Osheen

I was hunting with my father, Finn, and his warriors, by the shores of Lough Lein, when we saw the horse approaching. We knew at once that this was no ordinary happening, for the horse came over the water as smoothly as a swan.

The rider was a woman. My father greeted her with a respectful nod of his head. 'You are welcome, my lady. May I ask where you are from, and whether we can help you in any way?'

'My name is Naimh*,' she replied to Finn's question. 'I am from Tir Na nOg, the Land of Youth, and I would like to speak to your son, Oisin.' And then she looked at me directly.

I have not described the woman on the horse. It is not her beauty I remember from that first meeting - although she was, indeed, beautiful - but rather the way she spoke my name. She said that she had looked at me often from afar, and that she admired me as a poet and a warrior. For seven years, Naimh said, she had been longing to see me face to face, but those who live in the Land of Youth are invisible in the human world, so this had not been possible.

'Only now,' she said, 'after I have refused many offers of marriage, has my father agreed to let me ask you to come away with me, Oisin. In Tir Na nOg you will have all the honour and land of a great prince. There the crops never fail, the cup of wine is never empty. The people make music and dance, for there is no sickness of body and you shall be forever young. I could say many things about my country, Oisin, but words are not enough - let me share with you the joy of being there.'

For as long as I listened to Naimh, the shores of Lough Lein seemed like an enchanted place. I heard no other sound but her voice; not the screech of a wildfowl or the snort of a horse.

'Will you be with me in the Land of Youth, Oisin?'

'I will, until time is no more, my lady!' Then I mounted the white horse behind her, and we rode into the bright sky to the west.

That was the strangest journey of my life. Some of you may have had a dream, perhaps, in which you fly on the back of a great white mare over land and sea.

* Naimh is pronounced Neeve

My journey to Tir Na nOg was like that. Sometimes I saw people below - fishers for salmon in the estuaries and peasants working the fields - but they never looked up as we went by, and I knew that they could not see us. I was a part of the Otherworld already. As we crossed the sea I saw strange phantoms in the mist. Naimh told me to be patient when I asked about them. We were almost there.

If you ask me what was the first wonderful thing I saw in Tir Na nOg, I might mention the crowds who were waiting to greet me with smiling faces; or the abundance of silver and gold; or the delightful proportions of the castle in the distance: but what I remember most is the light sky. In the country of my birth there are grey clouds and near horizons. Over there, a soft light bathed everything between me and the far hills - as if Tir Na nOg was situated in that glow one sees from afar when the rainbow meets a privileged patch of the earth.

'Look at this land, Oisin,' said Naimh. 'Once you dismount the years will be inconsequential things, and for you Time will have no meaning. Is it not beautiful? And will you not be happy here?' I replied that the land was beautiful, and that anyone must be happy here.

And yes, I was happy there. The company of Naimh would have been enough for me, and I had, besides, any number of sights and sounds and new experiences to satisfy both the poet and the adventurer in me. I knew nothing of hunger, or cruelty, or death. I am tempted to say that the years went by, but I saw no sign of them passing.

Yet I must say this: when I left the land of my birth I brought something with me - a deep, abiding power that I could not get rid of. I mean the power to remember. I could still see in my mind the face of my father. Sometimes I would use the power of memory to steal away for a meal with my companions and hear their laughter fill the room. I could even imagine the delight in the howls of my dogs if only they could see their master again. And there were times when I dreamed of our land in the grip of winter, and I would long to crack the ice over our well with my heel.

Think, those of you who are hearing my story - who would you be without the power to remember? Perhaps, after all, it is our memory that makes us who we are. You will understand that I had to ask Naimh to let me go back for just a short time. I wanted to see for myself how things were in the old world.

'Yes,' she said. 'But I don't want to lose you, Oisin.'

'You won't lose me,' I replied. 'I will come back with my mind at rest.'

Naimh gave me her white horse, the one which had brought us here, saying, 'You must not dismount, not for any reason. If you get off the horse you will never see me again. Please remember, Oisin, I will not be given the power to come and fetch you a second time.'

Then Naimh wished me a safe journey, and the white horse carried me home.

I had no clear idea what to expect there. Certainly I thought I might see my friends, no doubt older and wiser now than when we had hunted together. I wondered if my father would know me in his old age. You can imagine my disappointment when I found no trace of them, at first.

The very shape of the land seemed to have changed. Woods had been cleared, wells and even lakes had dried up. Farmers worked in fields where great stands of trees once grew. These farmers paused to look at me as I rode by, as if I were an object of curiosity. I tried to deny the foreboding in my heart as I headed for Ben Edair, the hill where I grew up, the homeland of Finn.

Only the shape of an old dwelling place was still there. Ivy, whins and bracken had conquered this place where hordes of hostile warriors had feared to walk.

In a glen close by I stopped to speak to some people who were struggling with a large stone. 'What happened up on Ben Edair?' I asked them. 'Do you know anything about the warriors who lived there? My name is Oisin, and my father was Finn, leader of the Fianna. I am trying to find him, or someone who knew him.'

My question astonished them, as their answer astonished me. 'My lord, we are confused. The heroes you speak of are from another time. We know them, of course, but only from the stories that are told about the great things they did many ages ago. But we are ordinary folk. Perhaps you will find others who can help you more than we can.' And so saying, they returned to shifting the stone.

They had helped me well enough. How long had I been in the Land of Youth? I had no way of knowing. Perhaps for a hundred lifetimes. Too long to see anyone I knew, or for them to see me.

On an impulse, thinking to help these people, I leaned over and pushed on the stone until it began to roll. As the saddle-girth snapped under the strain, I felt myself slip from the horse's back to the ground. And the great animal ran freely down the glen until it was out of sight.

It was returning to the place I would never see again. Left behind, the young Oisin – whom Naimh had loved for his power and grace and youth – began to feel in his very bones the weakness of extreme old age. Through dim eyes I saw my wrinkled, ancient hands, and I knew that I was mortal again. My lovely Naimh could not protect me now.

There is my story. I wait under the oaks that grow near Ben Edair. As surely as any leaf I will return to the ground when my time has come; or when Time has come for me.

LIMPET ROCK

For many storytellers the sea is a kind of Otherworld which has inspired a host of stories through the ages

John Fowler of Limpet Rock was known as a decent man who spread no gossip and did no harm. The thing that most shaped his life was a tragedy at sea when he was sixteen. A ferry boat between the islands went down in a storm, claiming the lives of his mother and father and his elder brother. After that he lived alone in a cottage built a little way back from the shore, not far from Limpet Rock.

There are people who are great in company - they can sing a song or tell a yarn as easily as blow their nose, but John Fowler was not one of those people. He didn't mix much. Alone in his boat he would fish the day long, although he often helped out a neighbour with the lambing or the harvest. On the whole he kept his own company, and whether he was lonely or not, or happy or not, people neither knew nor wondered.

One misty, clammy day he was gazing out of his window when he noticed something moving on Limpet Rock. This rock, whose rounded symmetry was pleasing to the eye, rose out of the sea like a gigantic upturned shell. You could reach it by walking when the tide went out. On the ocean side there was a shelf that sloped gently into the water, and it was not unusual for a seal to beach itself there in quiet weather.

These were not seals that John Fowler saw. A group of six or seven figures seemed to be sporting themselves, though it was hard to see anything other than shadows through the gloom. John put on his big coat and boots to go over for a closer look, but all he found on the Rock was a seal-skin abandoned near a pool. And a fine skin it was – there would be any number of takers if he produced such an article at the village market. The only worrying thing about his find was the fact that it shouldn't be there. John brought the skin back to the cottage, and after folding it carefully, he pushed it into a secret hole behind the chimney. Then he went back to wait in the shadow of Limpet Rock.

Some time went by. The tide was on the turn when he was surprised by the sight of a woman clambering over the rocks, clearly looking for something she could not find. Knowing that she was about to discover him, and not wanting her to think that he was spying, John stepped from his hiding place into view.

She shrank a few steps away, and shivered in the cold. Then quietly she asked him, 'Have you seen a seal-skin?'

'A seal-skin?' repeated John, not knowing what to think.

'Please tell me if you have seen a seal-skin.'

'It may have been washed away by the tide,' replied John.

When you say a lie, people hear a lie – this was what his mother had always taught him, and he knew it was true. The woman looked at him and said nothing. Her eyes were large and brown and wide-spaced. Night eyes, he thought, far-seeing eyes – she was wonderful to behold. John took off his big coat and set it round her shoulders.

'You'll be wanting some food. Come. I have hot soup.' When she hesitated, he added, 'We can't stay here, the tide will cut us off.'

The woman went back with him to the cottage, and there she remained. Around

the country went the word that John Fowler had found himself a foreign girl to be a wife, and wasn't it good for him to have a bit of company at last. People said that she was as quiet as John himself, and that they were well met. And there were children, too, as the years went by. One was a boy and the other a girl. Their father would bring them both to market on the back of a pony, and proudly talk about them to whoever would listen.

John Fowler never asked himself questions about this second event which had changed his life, this time so much for the better. He did not want to risk anything by thinking too deeply. The seal-skin was never mentioned. He was content to believe that a sort of bargain had been struck: the sea had taken one family away from him, the sea was paying him back with another.

Of course, if his wife had been deeply unhappy, he could not have borne it. But she seemed to be content for most of the time, and indeed, she seemed a lot more content than some of the bickering wives of other men he knew. This thought was a comfort to him whenever she stole away to Limpet Rock to stare across the ocean. From the window he would watch that motionless, windblown figure, and wonder what she was seeing. Where did her mind go? Did she know of a place where a ghostly kind of sunlight falls on palaces with sea-shell walls? Then he put such thoughts from his mind. He did not ask her why she went to the Rock. Part of her, he knew, would always be looking away.

Then a vicious gale blew up one spring, and caused damage to the roof. While John Fowler was outside inspecting the damage, his son explored the hole behind some bricks which had come loose in the chimney. He threw down to his sister the folded thing he found in there.

The little girl, who was six years old at this time, pressed the fur to her cheek and brought it to her mother.

'It's so soft, Mama.'

'What have you there, my sweet?'

'Douglas found it. Why is it so soft, Mama?'

The mother took the seal-skin with trembling hands. She hugged the children both and kissed them several times.

'Your daddy will be back soon. Be good, won't you? Don't go near the fire. Oh

48

my two wee lovelies, always be happy!' After one backward glance from the door, she was gone.

When John Fowler returned and saw the loose bricks, he let out a cry. 'Who's been up there?'

The children, startled, would not answer.

'Douglas, where is your mother?'

'She went out.'

'Where?' cried their father. 'What did she say?'

'She just said don't go near the fire.'

Out he rushed then, his heart thumping fit to burst as he lurched through the knee-deep turning tide. On the ledge he saw her. One long last look she gave him, and oh, the eyes of a seal can seem to know and feel so much! Then she slithered away into the deep.

John Fowler hoped she would come back to him, and a hope which is cherished can last for years and years. He reared the children, settling into a way of life that suited him. Sometimes a seal came close to the boat he was fishing from, especially when the children were with him. But he could never convince himself that this was she.

In old age he sometimes remembered that last look of the seal from Limpet Rock. What had those eyes meant to say to him? No doubt there had been something of tenderness there, and something of pain. But finally he understood that his lady of the sea had been saying, and saying forever, the word that cracks the heart. Farewell.

ETAIN'S OTHER WORLD

Etain was the wife of Eochy*, the most powerful of the Irish kings at the time of this story. They lived together in the great royal rath** called Tara, and Etain was well pleased with her life there. She had power and prestige; and she had, besides, the deep satisfaction that comes from knowing she was much loved.

But sometimes there were nights when Etain dreamed of another place. It was as if her mind had left her sleeping body and made a journey to a different world. Even during the hours of daylight she would hear snatches of strange music or catch a glimpse of something unfamiliar in a misty glen. At such moments she felt that she was standing in a kind of borderland. On this side was the world she knew; over

* Eochy is pronounced Yoch-ee
** Pre-historic hill fort

there was another world whose joy and pain she felt she half remembered . . .

One day a stranger appeared during an outdoor banquet on the slopes below Tara. As he approached, Etain wondered why he did not cause more of a stir among her companions, for the fellow had startling good looks. His clothes had been cut from material of the finest quality, and he wore them with the authority of a royal prince.

Then she realized with a start that this was no ordinary visitor. No one could see him but herself.

The stranger smiled briefly, then seemed to stare at her with a deep longing. 'I am the one who knows who you are,' he said quietly.

'I know who I am,' Etain replied evenly. 'I am the King's wife. But who are you, and where are you from?'

Again the stranger smiled, as if names and places were things of no importance. 'And does the King treat his wife well?'

'Since you make it your business to ask, he treats me as well as a wife could wish.'

'A man I know was married once,' the stranger went on, 'to someone he has never forgotten. But this man, Midir, was careless, and lost the wife he loved. A jealous woman put a spell on her and changed her into a butterfly with crimson wings. Even that was not enough. This evil one summoned up a wind that blew the butterfly out of the country so that Midir could never see her again. And he has never had peace of mind since.'

Etain glanced at the stranger. 'Things like that can only happen in the Otherworld,' she said. 'You seem to know this person called Midir very well. Is it you?'

'Yes. I am Midir.'

'And what happened to the butterfly?' Etain asked him.

'For seven years she was blown from one end of this land to the other. Until one day the wind blew her into the rafters of a great house. Far below, a family sat at table for their evening meal. Of course, the enchanted creature was exhausted by now, long past caring whether she lived or died. When she fell from the rafters into a drinking cup on the table, a woman sitting there drank the cup of wine, butterfly and all. Not long after this event, the woman gave birth to a baby girl who grew up in the likeness of the wife Midir had lost. The little girl grew up without knowing who she really was, although sometimes . . . sometimes she could see and hear more than human eyes could see and hear.' The stranger paused, and finished, 'Her name is Etain.'

Etain did not speak for some moments. She could not decide whether the story made her feel sorrowful or glad – or whether, indeed, she shouldn't laugh the whole thing away.

'Are you saying . . . that I was your wife at one time?'

The stranger nodded. Then he described the wonders of this other homeland, a place of marvels for the mind to be astonished by and the heart to cherish. And he asked Etain to come back with him.

'I will not,' she said. 'I am the King's wife, and I will stay with him.'

'What if he allowed you to return with me?' asked Midir.

'Then he would not love me as much as I think he does,' replied Etain. 'Now please go, and leave me with the peace of mind you say you are looking for.'

•   •   •

There the matter rested for some weeks. Although Etain tried to forget the magical story she had heard about her former life, the words of Midir returned to haunt her. She knew he would be back.

When Midir came once more to Tara, it was her husband he visited. Eochy was up early that morning, walking the circular ramparts of Tara, when a long-haired youth stepped into his path. The King's quick eye took note of the stranger's purple robe, his sword, his shield with its rivets of gold.

'My greetings to the King of Tara,' said the youth.

'I don't remember you,' replied Eochy, 'but welcome anyhow. Whose party are you with?'

'None, Majesty, but I have been told about your great love of board games and I would like to test you with a game of chess. If you agree to play me, and I lose, I will pay you a prize of fifty perfect horses. What do you say?'

It was an odd request. But Eochy, knowing the strength of his own game, agreed to play. And he won. At the end of the game Midir slipped away, only to return the following morning with the horses he had promised, and with the offer of another game. The prize, he said, would be bigger still – cattle, sheep and boars.

This time Eochy won again. But he already believed that his opponent was not from the world of mortals, and for the third game's prize he demanded the impossible. 'If you lose, you will clear my valleys of stones, make the swamplands into good land and give me full grown trees on the bare hills. Agree to this and I'll play you.'

'Let it be so,' smiled Midir. 'My condition is only this: you must promise not to look out of the windows of Tara tonight, and see my people at work.'

'No one will watch,' said Eochy, 'not even the dogs will look out from Tara tonight.'

Eochy won for the third time. That night he placed spies in the walls and warned them to remember everything they saw. The spies looked on in amazement as a ghostly army of labourers descended on the marshes and hills around Tara. By dawn the landscape was transformed in the way that had been promised.

When Midir arrived in the morning there was no ready greeting from him and his eyes were cold with anger. Eochy saw that he knew about the spies.

'So much for the word of a king,' Midir said.

Eochy nodded an apology. 'No harm was meant, believe me, but let me make amends. You may set the stake for this morning's game.'

'This game is for an open stake,' said Midir. 'The winner may ask for whatever he likes, and the loser will grant his wish.'

They began to play. As the quiet minutes passed, Eochy dreaded to think what price he would have to pay if he lost this game. In spite of all his skill, the position of his pieces on the board grew worse and worse. At last he looked up at his opponent, and nodded.

'The game is yours. What is your stake?'

'One kiss from your wife,' came the astonishing reply. 'I want to hold her in my arms once more - the way I used to do when we loved one another in the Land of Youth.'

Eochy, rising from the table, tried to think clearly. The man was asking a monstrous favour. Yet he had given his word! 'Come back at the end of the month,' he said, 'and your stake will be honoured.'

Throughout that month Eochy made his preparations, for he knew that he

54

faced the awful prospect of losing Etain for ever. She had told him the story of Midir and the enchanted butterfly, and he believed it completely. One kiss! That fellow would never be content until he had lured Etain away from him. So Eochy sent messages to the kings and princes of Ireland to come to his aid. By the end of the month an army had gathered in the fields and valleys around the royal rath at Tara. The doors of the great hall were locked. Inside, Eochy and Etain sat surrounded by chiefs and warriors.

Even so, Midir appeared before them in the centre of the room. 'I am here to claim what you owe me,' he said calmly, 'by the rules we laid down.'

'By the rules, then,' Eochy agreed grimly. He could see nothing but hurt and pain at the end of all this.

Etain did not know what to think as Midir encircled her with his arms.

'Have no shame,' Midir whispered to her. 'You have not been disloyal to Eochy. But you come from a land beyond time, my sweet lady, and it is calling you home.'

She did not want to go, she did not want to stay. Or was it that her heart longed to go and yet longed to stay?

The others, powerless to do anything but watch, saw Etain and Midir rise into the light streaming from a great window near the roof. Then Eochy leapt to his feet with a cry and raced outside. With his warriors about him, and his chiefs and kings, he looked up and saw two swans together flying eastwards from Tara.

WEE JOHNNY'S REVENGE

*You have probably noticed from your reading that some
stories for children are strong stuff. In some of these stories
grown-ups do terrible things to children – think of some of
the wicked stepmothers you've read about, for example.
In this gruesome story Wee Johnny gets his own back
on his dreadful mother.*

Once there was a farmer who had a wife and a son and a daughter. He was very fond of the three of them and did his best to keep them all well fed, even if the times were hard. Anyway, one day he caught a good-sized hare, and took it home for his wife to cook.

While it was boiling away on the fire, the man's wife couldn't keep her hand out of the pot. She broke a bit off here and a bit off there and when she had eaten the whole thing clean away she began to wonder what to give her man for his tea. So she called Wee Johnny her son to come and get his hair combed, and while she was combing his hair she knocked him on the head and put him into the pot.

Her man came home and he said, 'How's the hare doin'?' and she said back to him, 'It's doin' rightly.'

They sat down to eat, and after a while the man came across a foot and he said, 'That looks very like the foot of my Wee Johnny.'

'Catch yourself on,' said the woman, 'that's the hare's foot you've got.'

Next the man came across a hand, and he said, 'That's surely my Wee Johnny's hand.'

'Your mind is wandering,' said the woman, 'that's another one of the hare's feet you've got.'

So they ate up their dinner, and when it was over Johnny's wee sister, Katy, gathered up the bones that were left and buried them in a hole outside the door. But the bones weren't content to just lie there - they grew and they grew when nobody was looking and eventually they grew into a pale white pigeon, which upped and flew away.

The pigeon flew on until it saw two women washing clothes in a stream, and it sang out to the women:

> 'Pew, pew,
> Me Mammy me slew
> Me Daddy me chew,
> And into a pigeon I grew and I grew.
> Then I took to my wings and away I flew.'

The song of the pale white pigeon made the women take pity on it. 'You poor bonny bird,' they said; and they gave it the clothes they were washing.

Then the pigeon flew on until it came to a man counting money in his garden. A heap of silver coins piled high was shining on the table, and the bird lighted on them.

> 'Pew, pew,
> Me Mammy me slew,
> Me Daddy me chew,
> And into a pigeon I grew and I grew.
> Then I took to my wings and away I flew.'

The song of the pigeon made the man take pity on it. 'You poor bonny bird,' he said; and he gave it all the money he was counting.

Then the pigeon flew on until it spied two millers grinding away at corn, and it started up its song again:

> 'Pew, pew,
> Me Mammy me slew,
> Me Daddy me chew,
> And into a pigeon I grew and I grew.
> Then I took to my wings and away I flew.'

The song of the pigeon made the millers take pity on it. 'You poor bonny bird,' said the millers; and they gave it the big millstone they had for the corn.

The pale white pigeon didn't waste a minute, he flew away back to his father's house and perched up there on the roof. Down the chimney he threw a scattering of pebbles and Katy came out to see what was the matter. When Katy came out, the pigeon threw down the clothes to her.

Some more pebbles went down the chimney. When the father came out, the pigeon threw all the silver at his feet.

Some more pebbles went down the chimney. When the door opened and the mother came out, she got the millstone fair and square dropped on her head, and that was the finish of her.

The pale white pigeon flew over the mountain and was seen no more. The honest farmer and his daughter lived long and happy after that and if they haven't died since, then they must be livin' still.

THE GREEN MAN

The great midwinter feast at Camelot was a grand affair. Anyone who thought he was important wanted to be there, for the host was none other than King Arthur himself. It was a glittering occasion for the great and the good of the land.

And it was fun! During the few hours of daylight, spectators with steaming breath screamed their support for the jousters and the swordsmen who battled with each other in the palace yards. Then they feasted on game from the royal forests, and after dark came dancing, the tricks of jesters, the soothing songs of minstrels and the cup of sweet mulled wine.

One year, an uninvited presence turned up at the great midwinter feast. Arthur had just welcomed his guests to the main hall, and was about to take his seat at the high table when the doors burst open and a wind swept through the room. It was followed by the clattering of hooves. Into the hall, stooping to enter, rode a monstrous figure on a prancing warhorse.

He was huge. But his size alone did not silence the entire company. He was *green*. Everything about him was green - his hair, his beard, his skin, his clothes, his very horse. In his right hand he carried a battle axe, and even the axe was green. Together, man and beast approached the high table.

'Who are you?' asked Arthur. 'We'll be happy to lay a place for you at table if you've come a long way.'

'Food is not what I'm looking for,' said the stranger, scarcely hiding his arrogance. 'I have a challenge for the bravest of King Arthur's warriors - the bravest of the brave. It is a matter of honour.'

'You can speak freely,' replied Arthur. 'Honour is something we understand, and a fair challenge will be met.'

'Then let the bravest man among you take my axe and slice off my head. I won't resist. In fact I'll make it easy for him by lying down. He will find that the head will come off neatly enough if his aim is good.' The green man paused, his eyes glinting in the flicker of the fire. 'All I ask is that in a year and a day from now, he allows me to do the same to him. He will submit to my axe without flinching.'

Now the warriors of Arthur's court were famous throughout the land. The idea of removing a head did not trouble them, even if it was *green*, for they had removed the heads of many dragons, trolls and evil knights. It was the last part of the bargain they didn't like the sound of. None of them wished to have his own head removed. They stared at the floor, they stared at the roof, they did anything but meet the mocking gaze of the green man, who got down from his horse.

'Where are the fearless warriors?' he taunted. 'I expected a queue to form and what do I find? A shifty-eyed bunch with no honour. Well?'

'I will accept your challenge,' said a voice from a side table. 'If all you want is someone to slice off your head, then it might as well be me.'

The speaker, Gawain, walked forward to take the axe from the green man, who lay down and pulled aside the curtain of hair from his neck.

'Are you sure about this?' asked Gawain.

'Strike!' came the reply. 'Unless my axe is too heavy for you.'

And indeed, the axe was heavy. Nevertheless, Gawain raised it high, and delivered a stroke which cut through muscle and bone and fetched a metal note from the stone below. The head squirted away towards the fire. Amid an appalled silence the green man rose to his feet, lifted his head by the hair and tucked it under his arm as if this was a cabbage he had just picked. Then he remounted.

And the severed head spoke! 'My business here is over. But you, sir' – he levelled the axe at Gawain – 'you will come and face me at the Green Chapel in the Wilderness of Wirral one year and a day from now, and you will submit to my axe without flinching. If you don't keep your word then you will die without honour, and people will choke when they speak your name.'

With a whirl and a clatter of hooves, the horse and headless rider left the hall. A buzz of conversation began, which quickly became a rising tide of excitement and dismay as people tried to make sense out of what they had seen.

'This was a good trick,' Arthur called out, determined to have calm. 'It was an illusion, some kind of clever entertainment arranged for us. The play-acting is over, let the banquet begin!' And he signalled for the servants to bring food.

Late that evening, when most of the company had gone to bed, Gawain came to sit with Arthur and his dogs beside the fire. They talked about trivial things before Gawain lowered his voice to say what he was really thinking.

'I felt the blade go through his neck. If that was a piece of play-acting it's the best I've ever seen.'

Arthur nodded. 'Someone, or some*thing*, is putting us to the test. Perhaps this was one challenge we should have ignored.'

'But I didn't ignore it,' Gawain pointed out. 'I cut off his head! And by doing it I gave him the right to cut off mine. Am I honour-bound to do as he says?'

'We're all bound by the words we speak,' replied Arthur, choosing to stare into the fire rather than look directly at Gawain. 'I see nothing else for you but to submit to his terms.'

The winter passed. With the coming of spring there began again the serious pursuit of outdoor pleasures. For the warriors of Camelot this meant chasing a wild-eyed stag through the woods, stalking a dangerous troll in its dark hideaway, or walking in the gardens of Camelot with someone pleasing on your arm. No one gave a second thought to the green man on his plunging warhorse.

No one but Gawain. Throughout the summer he took no pleasure in the things that pleased other people and had once pleased him. The yellowing of the leaves in early autumn reminded him that time was passing quickly. In his dreams, again and again he raised the axe and brought it down, and watched that green spectre gallop from the great hall with his still-talking head wedged under his arm. The other side of the bargain – his side of the bargain – he could hardly bear to think about. He had been given the time and place of a meeting he could not avoid: an appointment with his own death.

When the time for the midwinter feast at Camelot arrived once more, Gawain was not among the company. He spent the shortest days of the year travelling north, seeking the Green Chapel in the Wilderness of Wirral. The ground beneath his horse was flinty with frost and neither man nor beast stirred under a wintry sky that promised snow. Sometimes he knocked on a cottage door to ask where he was, but for the most part he received only a look as cold as the weather – until at last someone directed him to a long ravine at the foot of the mountains.

The chapel he found there had been hewn from the very rock. The mouth of this place, overgrown with green moss, made it seem more suitable for a company of wolves than for a human being. But then, Gawain reflected grimly, whoever waited in there was something more – or perhaps less – than human. He dismounted and walked in.

There stood the green presence, stroking his axe as if it were a love object. Thankful for small mercies, Gawain noted that the head was back where it belonged.

'Ah! My guest has arrived,' said the green man. 'It's the proper thing to do, you know. Nothing lives after a man but his honour.'

'Let's get on with it,' said Gawain.

He lay down and bared his neck. Seeing a shadow on the wall, he knew it was the green axe rising up to come down again. He closed his eyes but felt the rush of air as it missed his head and thudded into the gravel soil beside his ear.

'You moved, knight,' the green man said. 'I saw your whole body twitch.'

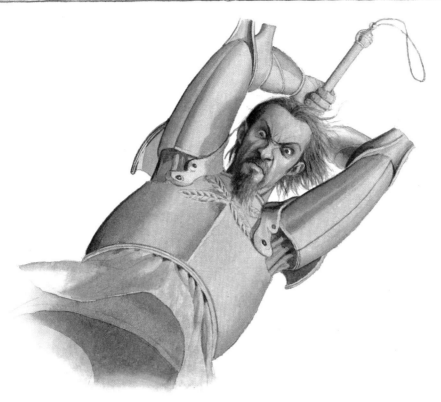

'A moment's weakness of the flesh,' said Gawain. 'Strike again and be done with it!'

Once more the axe came down, once more it missed its mark and again the green man spoke. 'You flinched, knight. There must be no fear, that was the bargain.'

The man was toying with him! And no doubt enjoying it, too. Gawain, suddenly full of contempt for this enemy, and burning with rage at himself that he should be so helpless, stiffened his body for a third blow - which duly came. The axe head stopped at his neck, the blade just grazing his skin. Gawain leapt to his feet, sword in hand.

'The blow was taken without fear and the challenge has been answered. Defend yourself, sir, whoever you are - the game is over.'

But it was no longer the green man who faced him in the dim cave light. He saw a stranger no taller than himself, leaning on a battleaxe of normal size.

'Put up your sword,' he said. 'My name is Bertilak, I live in a valley to the west of the mountains and I had no choice in this matter, any more than you had. A shape-changer called Morgan Le Fay came into my castle and put me under a spell to challenge the knights at Camelot.'

'Why?' asked Gawain.

'Who knows the mind of a shape-changer!' declared Bertilak. 'I think it was to bring shame on you all – no one would meet the challenge, she thought, or the one who accepted it would run away from the certainty of death.' Bertilak paused, and smiled. 'But you would not run. And now we can both go back to the way we were.'

Gawain's return across the Wilderness of Wirral was a journey he had not expected to make. Neither the cold nor the steadily falling snow bothered him now. Soon the year would be on the turn, he thought – the spring was coming. Once again he would take pleasure in the things that used to please him, only this time with the added joy of someone who has been granted a second life.

LITTLE FAWN

The importance of animals in human life has been fully recognized by storytellers through the ages. Sometimes the animals are magical, terrifying creatures, but just as often they are described as loyal and much-loved servants of their human masters.

Animals play an important part in the next two stories. In the first one we meet an old and strange idea – that a wild animal can care for a human child. The hero of the second story is a dog.

It had been a good day, and now they were returning home by the light of a low sun. The dogs loped along in front, followed through the clumps of heather by Finn and his warriors on their weary horses. It was as if the entire hunting party of animals and men understood that the day's sport was over: ahead of them were food and the comforts of home.

What a surprise, then, when a fawn suddenly broke cover – and no more than a spear's throw away! Boldly she stared back at the hunting party, as if to challenge them to give chase; and then with a light little skip she was off through the heather, heading for the woods in the valley below.

The cry went up and the chase was on. The fawn, being fresh, easily outran all of the dogs except two, and Finn's companions soon decided that such a skinny little thing seemed hardly worth the risk of injury to their tired horses. 'Let it be, Finn,' they said. 'Too much effort for too little meat.'

But the two dogs, whose names were Bran and Skolawn, would not be recalled. Finn was obliged to follow them, and after a dash to the edge of the wood he came upon a sight that brought him to a halt in a mood of quiet wonder. His dogs – both fierce and noble beasts – had caught up with the fawn. Their lust to chase and kill had been transformed into something else entirely, for they licked the young deer's head and pranced around her like puppies who have discovered a new thing to play with. Then they followed Finn home with the fawn between, and allowed the creature to lie down with them at the fire.

It was an amazing sight to watch the three of them together. Finn doubted whether Bran and Skolawn would let even *him* approach their new friend.

That night as Finn lay in bed he became aware of a presence in the room. The maiden he saw there was so perfect in all her parts that she might have stepped out from his dream-sleep – but her soft voice was real enough.

'My name is Saba,' she said. 'And Finn, I am the fawn you chased this evening. I have been that fawn for three years because I would not marry the Dark One in my other life. But a friend told me that if I reached the home of the great warrior Finn, my enchanter would have no power over me. So here I stand as you see me now, to ask for your protection.'

Here was a story, thought Finn, well suited to the time of night! The moon, unmasked by passing clouds, suddenly flooded a patch of the room with obscure light.

'This Dark One,' asked Finn, 'did he put on you the shape of the fawn?'

'Yes. He said it would be with me forever. Or until I be his wife.'

'Let it be neither,' said Finn, for the warriors of the Fianna could not refuse help to the helpless. 'You can stay here as long as you like.'

In this way Saba came to live in the domain of Finn, which she dared not leave for fear of the Dark One.

Finn grew more and more fond of Saba as the weeks went by, and it was no surprise to anyone when they were married. In the months after his wedding, Finn's way of life changed completely. He gave up hunting because Saba could

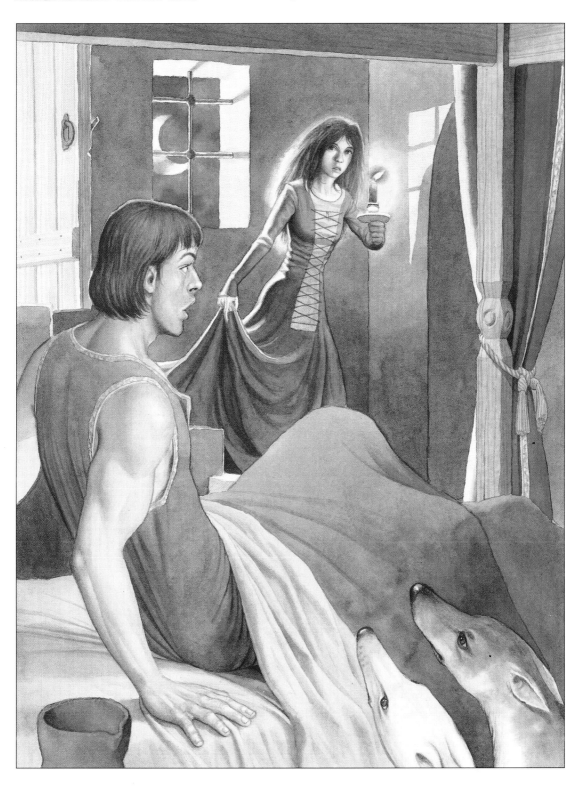

not hunt with him. He gave up visits to the local chieftains because she must remain behind. It was as if his happiness now depended completely on one person, and this all-consuming love made some of his friends uneasy, for it seemed to them that Finn, like his wife, had become a prisoner in his own domain.

But one day came news that Finn could not ignore. Pirates had landed on the eastern coast. Villages were under attack, the homes within them burning, and the year's harvest of crops stood at risk in the fields. The war-host of the Fianna gathered to deal with the invasion; and Finn must lead them.

'Be careful,' he said to Saba. 'Don't wander far and always have my servants with you. This is a short farewell, my lady – I may be gone three days, perhaps four.'

The pirates were an evil bunch but two or three encounters with the Fianna persuaded them back to sea again. Then Finn turned for the trek home, leaving a small force to deal with any pirates who might return. As he approached his rath on the Hill of Allen he quickened his horse, hoping for an early sight of his sloe-eyed Saba on the distant ramparts; but there was no sign of her. And there was still no sign of her when he crossed the ditch into the rath.

'Where is she?' asked Finn, although he feared the worst. She was gone, surely! None of his servants would look him in the eye.

'We did what we could, master,' one of them said, 'but you must understand what we were up against. Only yesterday you yourself came to the bottom of the hill, you with Bran and Skolawn, and the lady Saba ran to greet you.'

'I was a full day's ride away from here!' cried Finn.

'But it was your very likeness, master! And when Saba reached the far ditch she saw the danger she was in, but too late. The figure who was you became a stranger in a dark cloak, and your wife became a fawn. We looked for them until nightfall and we have been searching for them since, but there is no trace of the dogs, or the fawn, or the dark druid who pretended to be you.'

•   •   •

For seven years after that day Finn rode the hills and the glens and the plains of Ireland looking for the deer that was Saba. With him ran Bran and Skolawn; but even with their help he never found her. At last he accepted that the loss of her was permanent. His period of mourning was over, the search must be abandoned.

It was time to take up his old life again. Thus resolved Finn; but he had no way of knowing that the story of Saba was not quite ended.

They were hunting one day on the slopes of Ben Gulban when the dog-pack suddenly darted into a crevice. There, on the wild mountain, they discovered a young boy on his own. Whether the dogs or their masters were the more surprised it would be hard to say, for the boy seemed no more than seven or eight years old. Curiously, he gave no sign of being afraid, even when Bran and Skolawn approached to lick his face.

Finn got off his horse. He remembered this behaviour. Bran and Skolawn had been like this with the wild fawn.

'Who are you, boy?' asked Finn. 'How did you get here?'

He wouldn't answer. Rather than leave him on the mountain, Finn set him on a horse and brought him back to the Hill of Allen. Here, they discovered that he *couldn't* answer - the boy had not one word of any language other than the

grunts of a beast. They watched him eat. When he ate he stuffed food into his mouth as if he would never see food again. They watched him move. By using his arms as legs, he could scuttle about like a crab.

'You're a puzzle to me, boy,' Finn said to him. 'And no doubt I'm a bigger puzzle to you.' He wondered if the wild little thing had ever set eyes on people before.

The "wild little thing" turned out to have a gift for learning. From the beginning he loved the naming of things. He used words, as if they were magical keys, to escape from the silence of the animal he had been. Finn watched this happen, knowing that one day the boy would tell his story; and one day, he did.

'My first home was in a quiet little glen with a quick stream running through it. I never knew a mother or a father while I lived there. There was a man I used to see sometimes – a tall dark one, and perhaps it was he who left food in the caves where I slept at night, but I don't think so. It was the fawn who really looked after me, who kept me warm, who never left me, who was my teacher and my guardian, my mother, brother, father, friend. She had such love for me, I see that now. The fawn was afraid of the dark one. One day he came to the valley, and she made him so angry by running away that in a fit of rage he charmed her with a hazel rod, and she had to follow him. She kept looking back at me, but I had a spell on me too. I couldn't move. The next time I woke up I was in another place, where you found me, and the valley was gone. It may be beyond the mountain or within the mountain. I don't believe that I can go back there again. Or that I will see the fawn again.'

Finn set the boy on his knee, noting once more how the child had Saba's sloe-eyes and her tiny neat ears. From the beginning he had suspected a story something like this. 'We let our fawn slip away from us,' he said quietly. 'But I have no doubt she meant you to live here, with me, as my son. And the name you will carry in memory of her is Oisin – my Little Fawn.'

The boy grew up to become one of the champions of the Fianna. But he was more than a warrior. Oisin's abiding love of language made him the greatest poet and storyteller of his time, even though his first words were sounds of the wild.

GELERT

It's a strange thing about dogs, how we are able to love them. It matters not whether we are man, woman or child, we grieve for our dogs when they die. And whether his master is a poor man or a lord matters little to the dog, for in his eyes the one who owns him is a king.

It was a king who owned the great hound called Gelert - a large, grey, free-running animal with whom his master used to hunt in Snowdonia. Now there are many hounds who adore only one master and seem keen to eat everyone else; but Gelert, being the sort of dog who liked people, was allowed to wander freely about the castle of King Llewellyn. He could be seen snuffling and dreaming by the fire in the great hall, or lurking craftily near the kitchens, or patiently enduring the attentions of the King's older children. At night Llewellyn used to let him out to mark his territory, for there was a forest on the southern side from which a half-starved wolf would sometimes stray.

One day in early spring, Llewellyn assembled his horses and hounds for a morning in the hills. The ground was far from perfect underfoot, but the King was determined to ride. Bad weather had kept everyone shut indoors for almost a month, and then there had been the celebrations following the birth of another royal baby. Llewellyn, itching to be away, called out to the huntsman.

'What's keeping you?'

'There is no sign of Gelert, Majesty,' came the reply. 'He hasn't answered the call.'

It was strange to be waiting for Gelert, who loved the hunt more than his dinner. Ahead of the horses he would follow any quarry through thick and thin, then return filthy and bedraggled, but somehow never quite exhausted.

'If he's not here he's not here,' said Llewellyn. 'Start without him.'

It wasn't a successful hunt. They put up the occasional hare, but the dogs found it hard to slop their way through waterlogged ground after the thaw. Now and then Llewellyn wondered where Gelert might be. After two useless pursuits he decided to go home, content with the thought that at least they'd had a run. Soon the weather would turn and the land become firm again.

On his way to change into dry clothes, the King heard a whimper from the top of the stone stairs. He saw Gelert sitting there with his head hanging low.

'Yes!' cried the King. 'Ashamed, are you? I should think so - taking it easy while the rest of us do all the work. You're getting soft, that's your trouble.'

The dog struggled to its feet, and only now did Llewellyn see the matted blood on its coat. There was more blood - a long smear of it led from the quiet annexe where the infant rested in his crib; and already the panic in Llewellyn was rising. He rushed in there, fearing the worst and seeing the worst in all its horror, for the crib had been knocked over, it was empty, the pale covers stained darkly red.

Ah dear God, where was the child, whose was the blood? Something unspeakable had happened here.

The dog had followed him in. Llewellyn stared into its full brown eyes. He saw the redness round the gums and his heart lurched. Too much trust, he'd given to

this monster, too much freedom. Sickened to see it still alive after the awful thing it must have done - and filled with grief and fury - he killed it with his sword.

Only moments later he heard a cry from an adjoining room. Rushing in there, he found the baby lying on the floor beside the body of a massive wolf. Llewellyn was relieved to find the child completely unharmed, but in the room itself not a piece of furniture remained standing. There were tattered clothes, broken pots and strewn flowers, and everywhere the tackiness of clotted blood. What a struggle there must have been here!

After the relief came the remorse. Oh, to turn back time and have the last few minutes over again! Llewellyn looked once more at the dead hound. This time he saw the torn ear and the gash in the throat. Only a moment's wait would have let the world's worst fool see that this dog had been involved in a fight to the death. The noble creature had saved his child. And then he had killed it.

Llewellyn had Gelert buried in a grave marked with stones. He did this to remind himself of the lessons a dumb animal had taught him about loyalty and love, and the dangers of blind rage.

THE SEEING EYE

Stories about fairies have been told in all parts of Britain for hundreds of years. The fairies of the Celtic imagination are not dainty little things with pretty wings - far from it. In the stories you will often find that people are afraid of the harm fairies can do in the human world. This Welsh story about a close encounter with a fairy is typical, and something like it is told from the north of England to Cornwall.

Once there was a farmer's wife who found the daily chores too much for her, now that she was getting old. After milking in the early morning and cooking all day long, she then had to sit and spin for hours until the candle burned low and the fire went out.

'At my time of life I could do with a bit of help,' she said to her husband. 'We'll go to the next hiring fair* at Caernarfon and pay a girl to come and live with us.'

'How much would she cost?' asked her husband, who was a careful man with money.

'Only what it takes to feed her,' replied his wife, 'and if I teach her how to spin

* Hiring fairs were common in those days. Older children left home to work - for example, on farms - in return for lodgings and a small wage.

we might even have a few pennies more. There's many a nice quiet girl who would be glad of a good home.'

With this object in mind they went to the next hiring fair, where they found a number of girls willing to take work as servants. The old woman, seeing a thin girl with yellowish hair standing a little apart from the others, approached her with the offer of a placement. She described the farm and the kind of work that might be expected, and assured the girl that they were good people who would treat her well.

'And from time to time we'll give you something to spend on yourself,' she added to clinch the bargain. 'What is your name?'

'Eilian.'

'Well you could do a whole lot worse than come with us, Eilian. My name is Rowena, and this is my husband Robert.'

After a pause, and with a shy nod of her head, the girl accepted the offer of work.

To begin with Eilian was everything that Rowena had wished for. She fetched water, minded the stove, kept the place well cleaned; and in spite of her thin looks she was a tough little thing and not a bit afraid to split logs with the axe. When to all this was added the girl's quick skill at spinning thread, Rowena felt that her choice had been a good one.

After some weeks, however, Eilian developed an odd habit. On clear evenings she would carry her heads of lint into the meadows and spin by the light of the moon. And when she came home from these excursions, she brought back far more thread than she could spin on the nights she stayed in. It was a mystery.

Out of curiosity the old woman followed her one evening, and found her dancing inside the circular remains of an ancient rath. To look at the girl one would have thought this was a crowded ballroom and that there must be music in the air; but in the hush of night she danced all by herself under the moon and stars. Rowena crept away, wondering how to make sense of what she had seen. When Eilian returned that night she had more thread than the old woman could spin in a week.

'It's strange, the way she goes out,' Rowena said to her husband one evening.

'Probably she's lonely, that's all,' he replied. 'Maybe she's from a big family and misses the company.'

'Well I can't think why she loves that moon so much,' grumbled the old woman. 'She'll not be much company for *us* if this is how she's going to be.'

Eilian did not come home that night – she never came home again. No trace of her was found when neighbours searched the local wells and all the fields around. She must have run away back to her family, people said. It was a mystery to the old couple why Eilian should break the bond she'd given at the hiring fair, for they had been kind to her. But what could they do except put the affair out of their heads and go back to the way they were?

Now the old woman had a good reputation as a midwife in that area. She had many years of experience with helping women at the birth of their babies, and her services were often required at short notice. It was no surprise, then, when a man arrived at the farm one night and asked her to come and attend his wife. He was a well-dressed man with a pleasant speaking voice and the good manners of a gentleman. Rowena went with him willingly on the back of his horse, although the man was a stranger.

They rode a rough and winding path to the summit of the moor, where a mound came into view. This mound was lightly crowned by a pale mist, and Rowena found herself wondering where on earth the man lived. How could anyone think of building a house in such a wild and lonely place? It seemed fit only for sheep! Then she saw the entrance to a cave. And within that cave there glowed an interior light.

'You will find my wife inside,' the stranger said. 'Please go through and I will join you shortly.'

It was a wonderful room. Rowena had heard how wealthy people live – how they have deep soft carpets and the best of furniture and ornaments of sparkling glass: now for the first time, she saw them with her own eyes. Even the bed where the lady lay was hung with silken curtains and draped with matching covers. It was as if she had been called out to be midwife to a queen.

This was a peculiar business! *Perhaps I shouldn't have come*, thought Rowena. But she had never refused help to anyone before, so how could she have said no?

Sometime during the night, the baby was born. As Rowena washed the child by the fire, the husband came to her with a jar of ointment.

'Please put a little of this on the baby's eyes,' he said.

'What is it? I've never anointed a baby's eyes before.'

'It is a special cream that we find useful. Only please remember this, for it is important - do not allow any of the cream into your own eyes. It will do them no good.'

It must be some sort of charm ointment, thought Rowena, who had her suspicions about this stranger from the moor. And these suspicions were proved true when, quite by accident, she rubbed her left eyelid with the same finger she had dipped in the ointment.

With that eye she saw how the magnificent room did not exist. The walls were the rough stone walls of an ordinary cave. The carpet was a plain dirt floor, and where the great marble hearth had stood before, now a small fire smouldered among blackened stones. Moreover, the wife who lay on a heap of dried rushes was her serving-girl, Eilian.

And yet with her other eye Rowena still saw the room in all its glory.

She gathered up her things as calmly as possible. 'I wish you luck and happiness with the baby, sir,' she said, 'but I have done all I can here and my husband will be missing me at home.' So saying, she smiled goodbye at Eilian as one would smile at a stranger, thinking it wise to hide from them what she had seen.

Her husband greeted her as if she had returned from the grave. To Rowena's amazement she been gone for three whole days - yet it felt to her like half a night's work. Her husband listened to the story of the cave and the ointment, and how that ointment gave you the seeing eye. Now at last they knew what had happened to Eilian. The lonely child had danced to the music of the fairy people, and gone away with them.

In the autumn of that year the old woman went to Caernarfon market to buy some dried flowers. She had a strange experience there. Out of her left eye she noticed a man strolling among the stalls. But out of her right eye she couldn't see him at all!

'Robert!' she said, pulling at her husband's sleeve. 'Look over there and tell me if you see the stranger from the moor. Eilian's husband!'

'I don't see him,' came the reply.

It's only me, then! thought Rowena. In all this busy crowd she alone could see him, and only with the eye she had rubbed with the ointment.

The stranger stopped at a stall that sold sandals. *Should I speak to him*! wondered Rowena. The crowd and the brightness of the day made her bold – the fairy mound was far from here.

'Good morning,' she said. 'Please could you tell me how is your baby? And is Eilian keeping well?'

The tall man turned and looked carefully into her face. 'They are both well,' he smiled. 'But I am surprised to see you. And even more surprised that you can see me. Tell me, is it one eye you use, or both?'

'This one,' said Rowena, pointing.

Then the stranger leaned towards her, and breathed on her eye with breath as cold as ice. When Rowena looked again she saw the buyers and the sellers in the market-place as before; but she could not see the stranger from the moor.

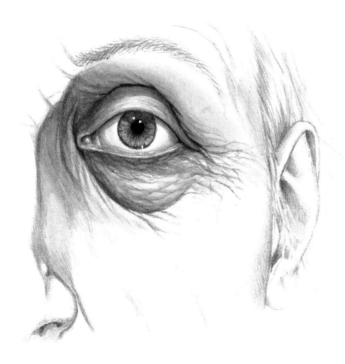

A FUTURE KING

In those days long ago, it was important for the king to have an heir. A king without a child was a worry to his advisers and to his subjects.

The advisers worried because no one was sure who would be the next king, and they knew that ambitious princes would scramble to sit on the throne when the king died. His subjects worried that the scramble for the throne would lead to a civil war in which they would have to fight. If the king had a child to rule after him, everyone knew where they stood.

King Pwyll* and his wife Rhiannon had no children. One day Pwyll's advisers approached him as a group to point out the need for a future king. Firmly, but

* Pwyll is pronounced Poo-ill

with respect, they gave examples of other kingdoms which had been torn apart by civil war, and they said that no one would fault the King if he replaced his wife with one who *would* bear him children.

Now Pwyll had no wish to take another wife - he and Rhiannon loved one another well. On the other hand he understood the main argument of his advisers, that a king must look to the future and think of the security of the realm.

'The Queen and I have been married for three years,' he replied. 'That's not such a long time, but if there is no sign of a child after one more year, I will agree to think most carefully about what you have said. Let us wait and see.'

To everyone's delight, the policy of patience worked. Rhiannon had a baby boy in the spring, and six nurses were chosen to be with her so that she and the future king should have the best of care. On the night after the birth, however, the baby disappeared. The nurses woke up to find Rhiannon sleeping in her bed - alone.

They looked everywhere for the child. How could a baby disappear! Mounting panic gave way to outright terror, for they knew that somehow they had lost the most precious thing in the whole kingdom. Someone would have to pay a price for this, and the nurses feared for their very lives. They saw that only one other person in the room could be blamed besides themselves; and that was the child's mother.

They took a puppy from a dog who had just whelped. They killed the pup, smeared Rhiannon with the fresh blood, and thus prepared the evidence for the story they would tell - that the Queen had slaughtered her own child in her sleep.

At the investigation which now followed, Rhiannon pleaded with the women to say what really happened, but they continued to accuse her. And in truth, she was easy to accuse. Weak from childbirth, stricken by the loss of the baby, and devastated that the blame should now fall on her, she seemed like a half-mad creature who could scarcely be relied on to remember what she had done.

'Majesty,' said Pwyll's advisers, 'it seems to us that these women have an explanation for what happened to the baby. It is a most horrible explanation, we grant you - no one wants to believe it, but Rhiannon cannot say where her baby is, she has no explanation at all. For the Queen to be innocent we have to take

the word of one woman against six. And since we find ourselves unable to do that, we are agreed that Rhiannon must be held guilty for what happened.'

'And her punishment?' asked the King.

'Execution, Majesty.'

Pwyll could not bring himself to accept the death of Rhiannon. Instead, she was ordered to sit each day for seven years by the horse-block at the gate of the castle, there to tell her story to every traveller who came by. Moreover, if that traveller wished to come up the hill into the castle, she must offer to carry him on her back. And such was the miserable life that Rhiannon led for almost seven years.

•   •   •

At the time of these events, one of Pwyll's subjects was a man called Teirnyon of Gwent. He was an honest man who had once been in the service of the King.

Now Teirnyon had a valuable mare in his stables which gave birth to a foal every year on the first of May. These foals would have added nicely to his income, were it not for the fact that they all disappeared as soon as they were born. In the morning he would find his mare lying in the hay – but no sign of the foal that should have been with her.

After losing a number of foals in this way, Teirnyon* decided that something must be done about the mysterious horse-thief. On the eve of May he strapped on his sword and lay down to wait on the stable straw. He observed the mare's labour and the birth of the foal. Then, as the new little creature struggled to its feet, Teirnyon heard the beginnings of a noise outside; and this unnatural noise was accompanied by a still more unnatural sight. A monstrous arm with fingers shaped like claws came through a window and seized the colt. Teirnyon, with the added strength of terror, swung his sword and cut off the arm at the elbow.

Outside the stables something screamed in the night. Rushing out to see whoever – or whatever – he had wounded, Teirnyon found that the owner of the arm had fled. Rather than stray into the dark woods he returned to the stables – only to discover a bundle of clothes lying in the doorway. And nestling in the clothes was a sleeping baby.

He carried the child indoors to his wife, who, after examining it for any sign of injury, declared that it was well. 'And it's a little boy, Teirnyon!'

Seeing his wife cuddling the baby, Teirnyon knew what she was thinking. They had never been blessed with a child of their own to care for. She kissed the pink little dimpled fingers.

'Perhaps this a gift to us, Teirnyon, a lovely gift.'

'I'd like to know who's giving it,' muttered Teirnyon. 'I don't think this is the child of a peasant family, look at the clothes he's wrapped up in.'

'But we must keep him,' said his wife. 'What else can we do? Think of this as a kind of payment for the foals you have lost. Of course we'll ask in the villages about him, but let us keep him while we may!'

So they kept the child. For six years they raised him; and besides his daily bread the boy enjoyed the steady love of two fond parents. Then, as was bound to

---

* Teirnyon is pronounced Teer-n-yon

happen, Teirnyon heard from a traveller the pitiful story of the King's wife - how she suffered at the castle gates for having killed her baby six years ago. In the light of this new knowledge, he began to watch his son closely.

'We have Pwyll's child,' he told his wife one evening.

'You can't know that, Teirnyon. He could have been anybody's, and now he's ours.'

'No. I knew the King, I remember him well. The boy has his features. And he is exactly the age the Queen's son would have been.'

'Who will ever know?' whispered his wife. 'We love him, Teirnyon, and he loves us and we deserve him.'

But she was too wise to hide from the truth. *They* would know. And the guilty knowledge would haunt them night and day. The boy was a future king and he must go back.

•   •   •

Presently Teirnyon came with his wife and adopted son to the court of King Pwyll. At the gate of the castle they were met by a woman who called out to them in a shrill voice. 'Are you going up the hill? I must ask if you would like me to carry you up the hill, it is my punishment.' And she added in a pathetic voice. 'They say I killed my own child with these hands.'

'No, my lady,' replied Teirnyon. 'None of us wishes to be carried.'

King Pwyll, who remembered the good services of Teirnyon in the past, made him very welcome. After wine and food had been brought for the three travellers, Teirnyon asked that the lady Rhiannon should be present at the table.

'Majesty, I have a story to tell,' said Teirnyon, 'and I would like her to be fetched up from the gate so that she can hear it, too.'

The story was told of the gruesome robber of new-born foals, and the leaving and finding of the boy-child on that spring night nearly seven years ago. 'Your royal son is not dead, Majesty - tell me if that is not your very likeness sitting there in front of you on an oak stool. And if it be so, then the Queen is innocent. I would only add that we kept the baby as our own son out of ignorance, and we cared for him as well as we could.'

In the quiet of the hall, no one seemed inclined to speak for some moments.

Then Teirnyon's wife touched Rhiannon on the arm. 'I wish he was mine, my lady, but he's not.'

'Oh if it were true!' said Rhiannon. 'All my trouble would be over.'

She framed the boy's face in her trembling hands, as if this were a fragile thing she held, like a flower; and she knew this was her son.

'I never gave you a name,' she whispered. 'Through all my trouble I dreamed of giving you a name.'

There were cries of acclamation from every corner of the room, and many who were present wept with Rhiannon and the King now that their misery was over. One of the chieftains suggested that the boy be known as "pryderi", meaning a great trouble or burden, as a reminder of the Queen's suffering and innocence. And this was what they agreed on. The young prince became Pryderi, son of Pwyll.

Pwyll himself, now turning to Teirnyon, asked him what gifts he would take for his part in all this; but Teirnyon shook his head. 'No gifts, Majesty. The boy's value to us cannot be measured, and we ask only to see him often.'

That wish was easily granted. Teirnyon's wife lived long enough to see the child she had fostered become king when Pwyll died. For many years Pryderi ruled over the seven Kingdoms of Dyfed in a way that pleased his advisers and subjects alike.

LAND OF GIANTS

*Legends of giants abound in all parts of Great Britain
and Ireland. These giants of long ago were as big as King Kong
and a lot nastier. One story tells how the first Britons defeated
a giant with the wonderful name of Gogmagog.*

There was a prophecy about young Britus even before he was born, and this prophecy had three parts. It was said that his parents would die because of him; that he would wander for years without a homeland of his own; and that one day he would rule in a remote and pleasant land. Now Britus's mother died while giving birth to him. And years later, when he killed his father in a tragic hunting accident, the first and second parts of the prophecy came true, for his grieving old grandfather sent him away from his homeland, never to return.

Although he came from a noble Trojan family (his grandfather had been carried from the ruined city of Troy), Britus roamed the seas like a common pirate. With his band of followers he sailed among the islands of the Mediterranean Sea, unable to settle down.

One day the wandering Trojans came ashore on a small island near the coast of Africa, where a grim scene met their eyes. Bodies of men, women and children littered the dusty tracks, and the crops of these farming people smouldered in the fields. There was no one left alive to say what had happened here. Towards evening Britus discovered a small temple dedicated to the moon-goddess and he made an offering there of blood and corn.

After nightfall the goddess herself appeared to Britus. 'You must not stay too long on the island,' she warned, 'this is not the homeland you have been looking for. You must sail west through the Pillars of Hercules into the sea near the edge of the world. The land you are looking for lies far to the north. It is a land of no extremes, without drought or famine.'

So the Trojans left the sea they knew so well and sailed through the Pillars of Hercules into the western ocean. Many of them were unhappy about the new venture. They worried about the storms and hidden rocks of these unfamiliar waters; but also they were haunted by the fear that every sailor carried with him: what if their ships plunged over the edge – and off the world! – in a fall that would last forever? During the long voyage north they kept the coastline of Iberia well in view, and often came ashore to find food and fresh water.

At one of these resting places the Trojans spent the night sleeping on a beach. In the morning they woke up surrounded by a party of warriors. The leader was armed only with a wooden club, but the club was the size of a small tree and the man himself was huge. Britus had never seen a more powerful-looking character.

'We are travelling north,' Britus called out. 'Once we have some water we'll be on our way without troubling you.'

'Those are Greek ships unless I'm mistaken,' came the reply.

'We are descendants of the people who fled from Troy. My name is Britus.'

'Well then, Britus of Troy, you will stay with us awhile and tell us your news.'

Although they were wary at first, Britus and his people soon relaxed, for they had come among friends who spoke the same language and remembered the same history – their ancestors, too, had fled from the blazing ruins of Troy. The huge man's name was Corin, and in the following weeks he became the friend of Britus. He said that his favourite pastime was wrestling with giants. He had wrestled with giants in many countries.

'I'm smaller than they are,' he joked, 'but quicker on my feet.'

'Where do they live, these giants?' asked Britus.

'Oh, in the hills and the caves under the hills. There aren't as many as there used to be, and the ones that are left are crafty.'

'Since you are still with us, I take it that you have never lost one of these contests.'

'Not yet,' grinned Corin, glancing up at the stars. 'Tell me about this great journey of yours. Do you want company?'

Britus considered the offer. They were sailing into the unknown. The strength of this big man might be useful. 'Yes, come north with us,' he replied. 'Wherever this place is, we'll find it together.'

For many days the small fleet voyaged north, keeping the coast of Gaul within sight on their eastern side. One morning they found they had left that mainland coast behind. The time for looking back was over; ahead of them, no more than a smudge in the milky distance, lay the outline of a promised land.

The Trojans came ashore in a natural harbour. In the weeks that followed no one came to challenge or to greet them. Scouting parties, searching for land to clear, brought back reports of green valleys and of wildlife thriving in the woods. This was, indeed, a lush and pleasant country – the only slight worry for the settlers was the fact that strange things began to happen. A hunter on his own would disappear and not be seen again, or a stone house would collapse in the night, killing the people inside. At first these mysterious deaths were blamed on carelessness or bad luck; until one afternoon, Corin and Britus came upon a sight that changed their minds.

They saw a ring of standing stones. From a distance the symmetry of this structure was remarkable – clearly, the stones had been placed there by someone and for a definite purpose; but when Britus came close and saw the true size of these things towering above his head, he could not believe that ordinary men had the power to do such work.

Who, then, had raised the stones?

'What *is* this place?' he asked, turning to Corin. 'What are we dealing with here?'

'Giants,' replied Corin. 'I've seen this kind of thing before, although never quite so . . . finished. It seems we might have company.'

'But where *are* they? I mean, there's no such thing as a small giant, surely they would be easy to see?'

'Not so,' said Corin. 'They can cloak themselves with clouds. A giant can stand as still as a tree trunk while a hundred men go marching by. He's patient, he's crafty, he will strike in the night.'

Britus glanced around, as if to check that no one was watching. 'We're in danger, then? They won't leave us in peace?'

'They'll leave us in pieces if they can,' smiled Corin. 'My guess is that they have attacked already. One blow from a giant's club would easily flatten a stone house.'

So, thought Britus – there was one final obstacle to overcome. If this land was meant for him, then he must win it. Very well, let it be so! He returned to the settlement to speak to his people and prepare them for battle.

In the struggle that followed Corin went looking for giants to wrestle with – it

was the big man's way of having fun. But the other Trojans sought to outwit the giants by covering deep pits with a framework of branches. This framework, strong enough to support a man, would give way under the weight of a giant, who was then easily dealt with.

The most awesome giant of them all was a two-headed monster named Gogmagog. Realizing that he and his followers were losing the struggle, he came down from the hills one day to settle this matter once and for all. He would challenge the champion of these invaders to a wrestling match, and after crushing his bones, drive the others into the sea. The thought of losing never occurred to Gogmagog, for, being the oldest of the giants and first-born of the earth, he possessed a special gift: so long as any part of his body touched the ground he could never tire or weaken. In short, he knew he was invincible.

When Corin accepted the challenge on behalf of the Trojans, he soon discovered that this giant was different from the others he had fought. Each time Gogmagog hit the ground with a mighty thump, up he rose fresher than before. Corin himself took a pounding from the giant's attacks. Although his skilful tricks kept him out of serious trouble, he felt himself slowing down. Gogmagog was winning.

'Soon my arms will be around you, stranger,' he cried out to the breathless Corin, 'you'll feel me hugging you to death. This is my land, the ground under my feet gives me its strength, my power is from Mother Earth!'

Now Corin knew why his opponent wouldn't tire. Instead of trying to hurl the giant to the ground, which only made him stronger, Corin lifted him high and held him there. At once the strength of Gogmagog began to ebb away. Though he roared and twisted to be free, he found himself carried to the edge of a great cliff. From here, Corin flung Gogmagog into the sea, which claimed him forever.

For the giants, the struggle was over. Those who remained alive retreated to the forests and the hills, and they have been in hiding ever since. The followers of Britus, who spread over the new land creating farms and villages, called themselves Trojans no more, but Britons.

INDEX